HEROES of World War II

Written by
Paul Beck and Anne Marie Walsh

7th WAR LOAN NOW..ALL TOGETHER

SCHOLASTIC

an imprint of
SCHOLASTIC
www.scholastic.com

Published by Tangerine Press, an imprint of Scholastic Inc.,
557 Broadway, New York, NY 10012
Scholastic Canada Ltd., Markham, Ontario

becker&mayer!
BOOK PRODUCERS

Heroes of World War II is produced by becker&mayer! LLC
11120 NE 33rd Place, Suite 101
Bellevue, WA 98004
www.beckermayer.com

If you have questions or comments about this product, please visit www.beckermayer.com/customerservice and click on Customer Service Request Form.

Authors: Paul Beck and Anne Marie Walsh
Editors: Betsy Henry Pringle and Dana Youlin
Designer: Sarah Baynes
Production coordinator: Tom Miller
Photo researchers: Katie del Rosario and Emily Zach
Illustrations on pages 30-31: Joshua Beach

Printed, manufactured, and assembled in Jefferson City, MO, 11/13

10 9 8 7 6 5 4 3 2 1

ISBN: 978-0-545-63748-0

13225

Heroes of World War II Image Credits: Every effort has been made to trace copyright holders. If any unintended omissions have been made, becker&mayer! would be pleased to add appropriate acknowledgments in future editions. Cover: Posters © Library of Congress; Daniel Inouye © Courtesy of the Associated Press; Jackie Cochran © Frank Scherschel/Time & Life Pictures/Getty Images; Charlie Dryden © Hulton Archive/Getty Images; Medical bag © Gary Ombler/Getty Images; British flag © Lightspring/Shutterstock. Page 1: Iwo Jima poster © Library of Congress; Advancing soldiers on D-Day © ASSOCIATED PRESS; Worker painting an aircraft © Library of Congress. Pages 4–5: Ruins of Rotterdam © Hugo Jaeger/Time & Life Pictures/Getty Images; Air raid shelter sign © William Vandivert/Time & Life Pictures/Getty Images; Army troops at training camp © Library of Congress; Battle of Britain commemorative stamp © Brendan Howard/Shutterstock; Decontamination squad, London © Keystone/Getty Images; Gas mask © Maciej Szubert/Dreamstime; "Hitler Wanted" headline © John Frost Newspaper Archive; French town after blitzkrieg © Popperfoto/Getty Images. Pages 6–7: German soldiers in Warsaw, 1939 © Getty Images; German invasion of Denmark, courtesy of the Freedom Museum, Copenhagen, Denmark; "Jood" patch © Courtesy of the Sydney Jewish Museum Collection, Donated by Mia Polak Meyer; Women in the Warsaw ghetto © USHMM Collection, courtesy of Sigmund Baum; Jews in the Warsaw ghetto © Courtesy of the Everett Collection; Map of German factory for sabotage, courtesy of the Museum of Danish Resistance; Polish rebel arrested by Gestapo © Mondadori/Getty Images; Bronze Star © R Carner/Shutterstock; Maria Gulovich Liu and companions © Seeley G. Mudd Manuscript Library, Princeton University. Pages 8–9: Hortense Daman, 1943, courtesy of Hachette Book Group, Inc.; Bicycle © Becky Stares/Shutterstock; Louvain, Belgium © Maxim Mayorov/Shutterstock; Nazis in Louvain, Belgium © Hulton Archive/Getty Images; "Child at War" by Mark Bles, courtesy of the Hachette Book Group; Order of Leopold © Kwasura/Wikimedia Commons; Ravensbruck concentration camp prisoners © Gamma-Keystone/Getty Images. Pages 10–11: Secretarial staff, Schindler Factory © USHMM Collection, courtesy of Leopold Page Photographic Collection; Schindler's list © Gamma-Rapho/Getty Images; Schindler at Nazi dinner party © USHMM Collection, courtesy of Leopold Page Photographic Collection; Labor papers for Cyrla Rosenzweig © USHMM Collection, courtesy of Janka Rosenzweig; Schindler in Jerusalem, 1970 © USHMM Collection, courtesy of Leopold Page Photographic Collection; "Schindler's Ark" by Thomas Keneally © Courtesy of Hodder & Stoughton Publishers; Schindler's List film poster © Courtesy of the Everett Collection. Pages 12–13: Irena Sendler © Courtesy of Janina Zgrzembska, via the Museum of the History of Polish Jews; Folded paper © bogdan ionescu/Shutterstock; Folded note © Ieneststan/Shutterstock; Jar © Kerry Garvey/Shutterstock; Jewish children, Warsaw ghetto © Al Steinkopf/ASSOCIATED PRESS; Ghetto badge, Poland © USHMM Collection, courtesy of Anna Hassa Jarosky and Peter Hassa; Jews in the Warsaw ghetto © Courtesy of the Everett Collection; "Life in a Jar" © Charlie Riedel/ASSOCIATED PRESS; Irena Sendler, 2007 © Alik Keplicz/ASSOCIATED PRESS. Pages 14–15: Raoul Wallenberg © Pressens Bild file/ASSOCIATED PRESS; Raoul Wallenberg at train station, Hungary © USHMM Collection, courtesy of Thomas Veres; Raoul Wallenberg © USHMM Collection, courtesy of Thomas Veres; Andras Galambos' Schutzpasse © USHMM Collection, courtesy of John Gerrard; Zelma Galambos' Schutzpasse © USHMM Collection, courtesy of John Gerrard; Raoul Wallenberg medal line art © Courtesy of the U.S. Mint & Treasury Department. Pages 16–17: Ten Boom Family © Courtesy of the Corrie ten Boom Museum, Haarlem, Holland; Oranje brassard © Imperial War Museum (IWM); Ten Boom Museum © Courtesy of Willem van Baalen; Corrie ten Boom and hiding place images © Courtesy of the Corrie ten Boom Museum. Pages 18–19: O.S.S. patch © Courtesy of the CIA Museum; William Donovan, WWI © ASSOCIATED PRESS; Donovan's whistle, WWI © Courtesy of the CIA Museum; O.S.S. monogram pin © Courtesy of the CIA Museum; Eileen Nearne © Courtesy of the Everett Collection; Nancy Wake honored © Adam Butler/ASSOCIATED PRESS; Virginia Hall portrait and identity papers © Courtesy of the CIA Museum, with permission of the Hall Family. Pages 20–21: Bletchley Park © Magnus Manske/Wikimedia Commons; Coded scarf © Courtesy of the Museum of Danish Resistance; Code deciphering commemorative stamp © catwalkers/Shutterstock; Codebreakers in Bletchley Park © Science & Society Picture Library/Getty Images; Enigma Machine © Courtesy of the CIA Museum; Alan Turing © National Portrait Gallery, London; Turing bombe © ALESSIA PIERDOMENICO/Corbis. Pages 22–23: London fireboat Massey Shaw returns © Popperfoto/Getty Images; Soldiers awaiting evacuation from Dunkirk © IWM; 2010 Anniversary of the Little Ships © Gareth Fuller/Press Association/Associated Press; Daily Sketch, 1940 © John Frost Newspaper Archive; Soldiers rescued from the water at Dunkirk © Hulton Archive/Getty Images; The Sundowner © Stavros1/Wikimedia Commons. Pages 24–25: Charlie Dryden © Hulton Archive/Getty Images; Tuskegee Airmen Class 43-C © Courtesy of the University of California Riverside Archives; John Rosemond's flight jacket © Courtesy of Mott's Military Museum; Keep Us Flying! © Library of Congress; Benjamin O. Davis © National Air and Space Museum, Smithsonian Institution; Tuskegee Airmen Congressional Medal of Honor © Ty Greenless/Dayton Daily News/ASSOCIATED PRESS. Pages 26–27: U.S.S. Helena, Pearl Harbor, 1941 © Courtesy of the United States Marine Corps (USMC); Remember December 7th! Poster © Library of Congress; U.S.S. Shaw, Pearl Harbor, 1941 © Courtesy of the USMC; Pearl Harbor commemorative stamp © catwalker/Shutterstock; U.S.S. Arizona remains © Boreccy/Dreamstime; U.S.S. Arizona and Pearl Harbor Memorial © Mpwood/Dreamstime; Japanese surrender, 1945 © Courtesy of the Naval History and Heritage Command; U.S.S. Missouri © Sergey Feingold/Dreamstime. Pages 28–29: Pilot Cornelia Fort portrait and flight log © Courtesy of Texas Womens University; Jackie Cochran's wings © National Air and Space Museum, Smithsonian Institution; Anne Armstrong McClellan © Peter Stackpole/Time & Life Pictures/Getty Images; Pilot Jackie Cochran © Frank Scherschel/Time & Life Pictures/Getty Images; WAVES recruitment posters © Courtesy of the Navy Art Collection, Naval History and Heritage Command. Pages 32–33: Uchida family © Courtesy of the Bancroft Library, University of California, Berkeley; Instructions to Japanese Americans © National Archives; Yoshiko and Keiko Uchida © Courtesy of the Bancroft Library, University of California, Berkeley; Iseri storefront window © Hulton-Deutsch Collection/Corbis; Little girl at internment transfer point © Clem Albers/CORBIS; Ansel Adams images of Manzanar © Library of Congress via Wikimedia Commons. Pages 34–35: Daniel Inouye, see cover; Rep. Daniel K. Inouye on campaign © Ralph Craine/Time & Life Picture/Getty Images; Nisei Soldier Congressional Medal of Honor, image courtesy George Hayashi, used with permission by the U.S. Mint & Treasury; 442nd Regiment © Eliot Elisofon/Time & Life Pictures/Getty Images; Nisei soldier Harry Koba in Italy © Courtesy of Densho and the Bainbridge Island Japanese American Community, from the Sakuma Family Collection. Pages 36–37: Mount Suribachi, Iwo Jima, Japan © United States Navy Photo via Wikimedia Commons; Flag raising at Iwo Jima © Courtesy of the USMC; WWII Marine Corps Memorial © Celso Diniz/Dreamstime; Iwo Jima postage stamp © John Kropewnicki/Dreamstime; Sergeant Michael Strank © Courtesy of the USMC; Private 1st Class Ira Hayes © ASSOCIATED PRESS; Corporal Harlon Block © Courtesy of the USMC; Private 1st Class Franklin Sousley © Courtesy of the USMC; Private 1st Class Rene Gagnon © ASSOCIATED PRESS; Pharmacist's Mate John Bradley © Courtesy of the USMC. Pages 38–39: Navajo Code Talkers Congressional Medal of Honor © Courtesy of the U.S. Mint & Treasury; Code Talkers © Courtesy of the USMC; Samuel Tso © Courtesy of the Tso Family; Navajo Rug, 1940s © Wikimedia Commons; CRI 43007 transmitter © Courtesy of ciphermachines.com; Code Talker © Courtesy of the USMC. Pages 40–41: Bataan poster © National Archives; 1st Lieutenant Josie Nesbit © Bettman/CORBIS; Nurse's bag, see cover; Zambales Mountains, Bataan Peninsula, Philippines © Samuel De Leon/Dreamstime; American POWs in Bataan © Courtesy of the Everett Collection; Fall of Bataan headlines, © National Archives; Angels of Bataan liberated, images courtesy of the U.S. Army Center for Military History. Pages 42–43: Susie Therp © Courtesy of Rosie the Riveter/WWII Home Front National Historic Park (NHP); Welder certification ID © Courtesy of Rosie the Riveter/WWII Home Front NHP; International Association of Machinists certificate ID © Courtesy of Rosie the Riveter/WWII Home Front NHP; Shipbuilding ID badge © Courtesy of Rosie the Riveter/WWII Home Front NHP; Workers in an aircraft © Library of Congress; Worker drilling rivets © Library of Congress; Women at Work poster © Library of Congress; Women worker commemorative stamp © catwalker/Shutterstock; Worker in an aircraft © Library of Congress. Pages 44–45: Rosie the Riveter © Rosie The Riveter" illustration provided by Curtis Licensing. For all non-book uses © SEPS. All Rights Reserved; Welders in a factory © Library of Congress; Workers © Library of Congress; Women worker recruiting poster © Library of Congress; ROHR Aircraft ID card © Courtesy of Rosie the Riveter/WWII Home Front NHP; Women at work in an aircraft © Library of Congress; We Can Do It! © Library of Congress. Pages 46–47: Save Scrap for Victory! Poster © Library of Congress; Children delivering scrap materials © Library of Congress; Is Your Trip Necessary? Poster © Library of Congress; Ration book © Courtesy of Rosie the Riveter/WWII Home Front NHP; Girls using rations © National Archives; Men in a Victory Garden © Courtesy of Rosie the Riveter/WWII Home Front NHP; Can All You Can! © Courtesy of the New Hampshire State Library. Pages 48–49: Faking hose seams © Constance Bannister Corp/Getty Images; Kristine Miller in bikini © Gamma-Keystone/Getty Images; Victory Suits © Keystone/Stringer/Getty Images; Foreign Ministers at the Inter-Allied Conference, London © Science & Society Picture Library/Getty Images. Pages 50–51: All posters © Library of Congress. Pages 52–53: War dog photos © Courtesy of the USMC; Silver Star © Natale Matteo/Dreamstime; Chips © National Archives; G.I. Joe © Press Association; PDSA Dickin medal © Courtesy of the Royal Green Jackets (Rifles) Museum; Wotjek © IWM; Corporal Edward Burckhardt with kitten, Iwo Jima, 1945 © CORBIS; Animal Guard brassard © IWM. Pages 54–55: Obstacles on Normandy beaches © IWM; U.S. soldiers, D-Day © National Archives; D-Day commemorative stamp, U.S. © catwalkers/Shutterstock; D-Day invasion beaches map © Courtesy of france-for-visitors.com; Operation Overlord © ASSOCIATED PRESS; Purple Heart © Gary Blakeley/Dreamstime; Aerial view of the invasion at Normandy © ASSOCIATED PRESS; D-Day commemorative stamp, UK © Brendan Howard/Shutterstock. Pages 56–57: Mauthausen flag artifact reproduction by Sarah Anderson, courtesy of the Word of Faith Christian School Holocaust Museum; Concentration camp liberation commemorative stamp © catwalker/Shutterstock; Freed prisoners at Mauthausen © USHMM Collection, courtesy of Ed Weinberger; Liberation at Mauthausen © UniversalImagesGroup/Getty Images; Women prisoners freed at Mauthausen © USHMM Collection, courtesy of Ray Buch; Postcard from Iwan Cohen © USHMM Collection, courtesy of Riwka Cohen; LeRoy Petersohn images, courtesy of Tricia Goyer. Pages 58–59: Private Harry Ettlinger © Hulton Archive/Getty Images; Portrait of a Woman with Ermine, by Leonardo da Vinci © Ccartoryski Museum, Cracow, Poland/Bridgeman; Discovery of a Fragonard among Nazi loot © Gamma-Keystone/Getty Images; General Dwight D. Eisenhower and the monuments men © Courtesy of the Everett Collection; Victory of Samothrace restored at the Louvre © Roger Viollet/Getty Images; Robert Posey's map © Topham/The Image Works; Mona Lisa restored at the Louvre © Robert Viollet/Getty Images. Pages 60–61: D-Day 50 year commemorative pin, courtesy of Peter Monaghan; D-Day 50 Years Memorial ceremony © Quadrillion/CORBIS; 1st Infantry Division monument © Tomasz Parys/Dreamstime; Fallen soldier tribute, D-Day © National Archives; Paratroopers on D-Day © ASSOCIATED PRESS. Pages 62–63: Adolf Hitler © INTERFOTO/Alamy; O.S.S. pin © Courtesy of the CIA Museum; Pearl Harbor attack © U.S. Navy/ASSOCIATED PRESS; Evacuation at Dunkirk © IWM/Getty Images; Distinguished Service Cross © Jim Barber/Shutterstock; First flag raising, Iwo Jima © Courtesy of the USMC; Stars and Stripes newspaper © Courtesy of Stars and Stripes; Sailer and nurse victory kiss commemorative stamp © catwalker/Shutterstock; Soldiers on the beach D-Day © IWM; Liberation of Mauthausen © Hulton Archive/Getty Images. Page 64: Victory pin, courtesy of George Hayashi; V-Day, Times Square © Bettmann/Corbis/ASSOCIATED PRESS; D-Day, Times Square © ASSOCIATED PRESS; Victory stamp © Boris15/Shutterstock; V-E Day © Bettman/Corbis/ASSOCIATED PRESS. Design elements from Shutterstock, unless otherwise noted: Banners © Kovacs Klaudia; Labels and elements © vso; Old photo frames © Valentin Agapov; Photo corners © Microstock Man. Additional medals shown throughout, courtesy of George Hayashi.

TABLE OF CONTENTS

PROLOGUE

World War II was the most destructive war in history. It began when Adolf Hitler's Nazi army invaded nearby countries in 1939.

Hortense Clews was an 11-year-old living happily in Belgium, when Hitler's forces took over her country. Her bicycle delivery job would soon make a difference in the lives of British soldiers behind enemy lines.

Samuel Tso lived with his family in the Navajo Nation near the Arizona–New Mexico border. Sam was 13 years old when World War II began in Europe. His native language soon helped him become a war hero.

Daniel Inouye was a 17-year-old medical helper in Hawaii when the United States entered the war. He joined the U.S. Army two years later. A "nisei" soldier, he served with other men born in America to Japanese parents.

As the war continued, the fighting spread to North Africa, the Pacific Islands, and parts of Asia. Millions were killed on three continents. Buildings, bridges, and railroads were all destroyed.

It took six years, but the U.S.-led Allied forces defeated their attackers, the Axis. Allied soldiers brought freedom to millions. They liberated Germany and Japan from cruel rulers.

During those dark times, Hortense, Sam, Daniel, and thousands more became true heroes. Here are their stories.

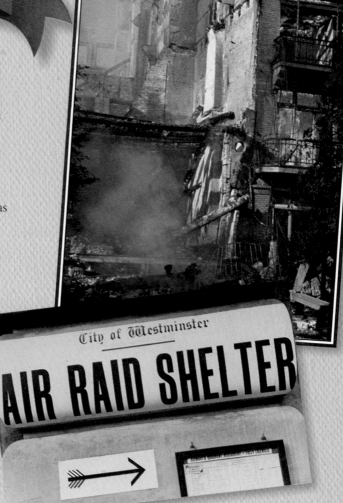

The streets of Rotterdam, Netherlands were a rubble after heavy German attack (top). Air raid shelters were located all over cities and towns to keep people safe during attacks (above).

Army troops marching during training.

Decontamination squad in gas masks.

A newspaper from September 4, 1939 calls Adolf Hitler out for his crimes.

German *blitzkrieg* left towns and cities in ruins.

LIGHTNING WAR

When Hitler's Nazi soldiers invaded their neighbors in 1939, they struck like lightning.

The Nazi army pushed through defenses quickly with machine-like force. Tanks, guns, and planes struck at the same time and kept pushing forward. By moving constantly without looking back, the attackers threw armies off balance.

From 1939–1941, *blitzkrieg* (German for "lightning war") tactics allowed Germany to overwhelm and occupy most of Europe. It seemed the heel of the Nazi boot would crush these countries. Then the tide turned.

OCCUPATION AND RESISTANCE

Nazi-Occupied Europe

After taking over Czechoslovakia and Poland, Hitler's forces occupied Denmark. Then they invaded Norway and attacked Holland, Belgium, Luxembourg, and France.

Nazi Germany was based on a racist idea that viewed Jewish people and other groups as "subhuman." Hitler's soldiers herded Jews into ghettos and took their homes and possessions. Jews in Germany and most occupied nations had to wear a yellow Star of David to identify themselves. People began disappearing and many starved or died from disease.

German soldiers marched through the streets of occupied cities (above). Jewish citizens were forced to wear badges to identify themselves (left).

Jewish prisoners being transported between prisons (left). Jews wait with their hands up during a Nazi search in the ghetto (above).

The Resistance

In occupied countries, the Nazi secret police, called the Gestapo, wanted people to spy on their neighbors to report anti-Nazi behavior. Still, many people risked their lives to resist the Nazi occupation. In every country, including Hitler's Nazi Germany, brave citizens joined underground movements. They passed along secret messages. They raided offices to get food coupons.

Some people sheltered Jews and other targets behind secret walls or in attics. Some served as spies to learn of enemy plans.

Others sabotaged the enemy. They carried arms or explosives to blow up weapons or storage facilities. Many rescued Allied soldiers caught behind enemy lines.

These activities were called the Resistance.

Resistance workers' plans to cut the power at a factory that repaired German airplane engines.

A Polish resistance worker is captured by the Germans.

Maria Gulovich

Maria Gulovich was a 23-year-old teacher when she joined the Resistance. She lived in the town of Hriňová in Slovakia. Maria spoke many languages and worked as a translator. She was also an underground messenger.

This work meant she had to move to a town where the Slovaks had risen up against the Nazis.

The Nazis wanted to punish the town with fires and shootings. Maria escaped with a group of American spies. They were working for the new the U.S. intelligence agency, the Office of Strategic Services (or O.S.S.).

Maria guided the escaping O.S.S. men through the snowy Tatra Mountains. For nine weeks, Maria, two British soldiers, and two American O.S.S. officers trudged through the cold winter. "Our eyebrows and hair turned to icicles," she said. They hid in a mine and a barn, but never felt safe. Eventually they reached safety.

Maria was awarded a Bronze Star from the American O.S.S. for her "ardent spirit devoted to freedom and justice."

Maria is on the far right.

Cycling for the Resistance

Hortense Daman Clews was 13 when she became a secret messenger for the Belgian resistance. Her hometown of Louvain was occupied by the Nazis in 1940. Hortense often delivered orders from her mother's grocery on her bicycle. But she also hid messages and dangerous explosives in the carrier basket attached to her bike.

Hortense was brave, strong, and clever enough to trick the enemy. She enjoyed outwitting the German occupiers.

When she was stopped and asked to empty her basket for a search, she kept calm. Once she offered two eggs from her basket to the Nazi officer. Eggs were scarce during the war. "Would you like them for tomorrow's breakfast? I must rush off home now as Mother will worry if I am late."

He took the eggs and off she went on her trusty bicycle. Beneath the eggs in her basket was a load of grenades.

Hortense and her family took many risks. They helped the Allied airmen to safety or back to England. She and her family rescued at least 36 British military this way.

Hortense Daman in 1943 (above). Her bike basket delivered messages and weapons to the Resistance.

The streets in Hortense's town today (left) and during the war (right).

Hortense's story became a book called *Child at War* in 1989. She was awarded the Order of Leopold medal from the Belgium government for her bravery.

Caught!

Then, in 1944, Hortense and her family were betrayed to the secret police. The Gestapo broke into their home.

Hortense was taken from her parents and questioned in Belgium's Little Prison. Her captors were looking for her brother. She would not tell them where he was. She left that prison alive because an Allied bomb destroyed part of it.

Without a trial, she was sentenced to death and sent to Ravensbrück Concentration Camp. But she was rescued by the Swedish Red Cross as the war ended. Hortense eventually returned home. On that same day, she met the British soldier she would marry. She was also reunited with her parents and brother. They had all survived.

Prisoners at Ravensbrück.

OSKAR SCHINDLER'S CHANGE OF HEART

All Oskar Schindler cared about was getting rich and having a good time. When the Nazis took over Poland, Schindler followed them there to reap the spoils. Schindler knew he could pay Jews low wages, so he opened a factory and hired many Jews. He was interested in making a profit and didn't care about the problems of his workers.

Then thousands of people in his city were loaded onto trains and taken to concentration camps—and Schindler learned that the Nazis planned to destroy every living soul in Poland who was Jewish.

Secretaries at Schindler's enamelware factory in Poland.

Beyond This Day

That's when Schindler had a change of heart. "Beyond this day, no thinking person could fail to see what would happen," he said later. "I was now resolved to do everything in my power to defeat the system."

At dinner parties, Schindler (singing with his arm raised) would cozy up to Nazi officers and trick them into divulging their plans. He bribed Gestapo officers with money and gave them forbidden goods in exchange for information about deportations.

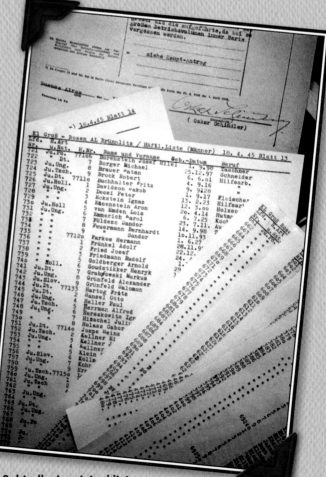

Schindler's original list.

Official papers for one of the women on Schindler's list.

STADT KRAKAU

Kennkarte Nr. 01664
Karta rozpoznawcza Nr

für den Juden – die Jüdin (dla żyda – żydówki)

Familienname:
nazwisko: *Rosenzweig*
                       Wiener

Bei Ehefrauen Geburtsname:
przy mężatkach nazwisko panieńskie:

Vorname: *Cyrla*
imię:

Zeigefinger (palec wskazujący):
linker   lewy
rechter   prawy

Rosenzweig Cyrla
Eigenhändige Unterschrift (podpis własnoręczny):

Besondere Kennzeichen (Znaki szczególowe):

Die Kennkarte ist nur gültig, wenn sie die zeitlich richtigen Gültigkeitsbestätigungen auf Seite 4, bzw. 6 enthält.

Karta rozpo... ... ważna, jeżeli czasowo obowiązując...

Every spring from 1961 until his death in 1974, Schindler went to Israel to visit the people he saved. He embraced their children as though they were his own family. In a way they were, because without him none of them would have been born.

The List

When he discovered his factory was going to be closed, Schindler moved it to a different city and made a list of 900 Jewish workers he wanted to work in it. He signed documents saying these workers had to work for him to help Germany win the war.

As time went by, Schindler added more names to his list, including children of workers. The people on his list were left alone by the Nazis.

By the end of the war, Schindler had saved more than 1,100 people. He had also spent his entire fortune. Millions of dollars had gone to bribe Nazis and buy supplies for his workers. Schindler and his wife fled to Argentina with some of the Jewish friends he had saved.

THE INTERNATIONAL BESTSELLER
Schindler's Ark
THOMAS KENEALLY
WINNER OF THE BOOKER PRIZE

Few other people knew about Schindler until a book based on his life, *Schindler's Ark*, was released in 1982. In 1993, the book was made into a film called *Schindler's List*.

11

IRENA SENDLER

Irena Sendler was a Catholic social worker in Poland. When nearly half a million Jews were forced into the Warsaw Ghetto, Irena joined the Polish underground movement called Żegota.

Irena used her position as a social worker to get into the Warsaw Ghetto to help Jewish children.

At first she brought food and medicine, but when families started getting deported, she worked to remove the children. She begged mothers to allow her to take their children out. Later people learned those who were deported were sent to death camps.

Irena and her ten loyal coworkers used many tricks to get the children out of the ghetto. They hid children under stretchers in ambulances. They placed small children in trunks, sacks, or suitcases and wheeled them out. They led children through underground pipes and secret tunnels.

Irena Sendler in her Red Cross uniform. Her job as social worker allowed her access to the Jewish ghetto.

Names in a Jar

Irena hid the children in orphanages, Catholic convents, and with families outside the city. The children were given non-Jewish names until the war was over. She wrote the children's real names on rolls of paper and hid them in jars buried under an apple tree in her neighbor's yard.

Irena filled jars with the names of rescued children from the Polish ghetto.

The Rescue

In 1943 Irena was betrayed. The Nazis sent her to prison. She was sentenced to death.

Now *she* had to be rescued. Her friends bribed the German who was supposed to shoot her. Twenty people helped in her rescue. The Nazis thought she had been executed. Instead she went into hiding.

When the war ended she dug up the jars in the yard. She worked very hard to reunite the rescued Jewish children with their parents or relatives.

Nazi soldiers taking Jews out of the Warsaw ghetto.

THE IRENA SENDLER PROJECT

Imagine meeting a real-life World War II hero!

That's what happened to Megan Stewart, Liz Cambers, Sabrina Coons, and Jessica Shelton. They were the students in Norman Conard's history class at Uniontown High School in Kansas when they rediscovered Irena.

They wrote a short play about her called "Life in a Jar." They performed it at their Uniontown High School. They traveled to Poland in 2001 to meet 90-year-old Irena.

The students also spoke with some of the children Irena saved, now grown up. They were interviewed on Polish television, and they performed their play.

Megan Stewart told a newspaper, "Irena wasn't even five feet tall. But she walked into the Warsaw Ghetto daily and faced certain death if she was caught. Her strength and courage showed us we can stand up for what we believe in."

The girls' play "Life in a Jar" has been performed 300 times all over the world. Its last line quotes the Jewish scripture:

"HE WHO SAVES ONE LIFE SAVES THE WORLD ENTIRE."

Saving the Jews of Hungary

Arrow Cross guards—Hungarian Nazis— were herding crowds of people onto a train. The people were Jewish, and the train was headed for a German concentration camp.

A man called out, "I'm Wallenberg, from the Swedish embassy. Anyone with a Swedish pass, step out of line." Some people stepped forward. The man told the guards, "You must also release all of those who lost their passes or couldn't pick them up in time." He had their names in his notebook, he said.

Wallenberg opened the notebook and began to read out names. His assistant went through the crowd whispering, "Raise your hands!" Hands went up. Wallenberg pretended to recognize people. "*There* you are! I've been looking for you," he would say. Or, "I remember giving you a pass just last week."

Wallenberg seemed official and knew how to give orders, so the Arrow Cross guards let him rescue 300 Jews. What the guards didn't know was that most of the Jews didn't have passes at all. The names Wallenberg "read" from his notebook were just common Hungarian Jewish names.

Swedish diplomat Raoul Wallenberg used his official position to save thousands of Jewish lives during the war.

Wallenberg (third from the right) on the train platform in Budapest, Hungary.

Diplomat with a Secret Mission

In 1944, the last large Jewish population in Europe lived in Hungary. Under the control of the Nazis, the Hungarian government began deporting Jews to German concentration camps. President Roosevelt and the U.S. government wanted someone to rescue these Jews. They chose Raoul Wallenberg.

Wallenberg was Swedish. Because Sweden was a neutral country, he could travel to Hungary as a diplomat. Once there, he did anything and everything he could to save Jews. He invented a special Swedish "Schutzpass" (German for "protection pass") and gave it out to as many Jews as he could. He told the Nazis that anyone who had a Schutzpass was under official Swedish protection.

In the end Wallenberg saved nearly 100,000 people.

Wallenberg mysteriously disappeared after being arrested by the Russians. He was suspected of being a German spy and was taken to Moscow. No one outside of Russia knows what happened to him after that.

Wallenberg's *shutzpass* rescued many Jews from death in the concentration camps.

A badge from the Danish resistance, called the Oranje.

ORANJE

The Ten Boom family: Betsie, Nollie, Casper, Willem, Cornelia, and Corrie

Hiding the Hunted

Corrie Ten Boom lived with her family in Haarlem, Holland. The Ten Booms opened their home to those in need. It became a hiding place for fugitives hunted by the Nazis. By protecting these people, the Ten Booms risked their lives.

The family hid both Jews and members of the Dutch underground. Some people would stay with them for long periods. Some would only stay for a few hours to rest while another "safe house" was found.

During the war, the Ten Booms and their friends sheltered 800 Jews and many members of the underground. Their bravery saved many lives.

The Ten Boom home in Haarlem, Holland is now a museum.

Searched but Not Found

Eventually someone betrayed the family. On February 28, 1944 the Ten Boom home was raided by the Gestapo. Corrie and her family were arrested.

The Gestapo searched the whole house. They suspected that Jews were being hidden by the family, but they couldn't find them. The Jewish people were safely hidden in a secret room behind Corrie's bedroom.

But the Gestapo found extra ration cards and materials from the Dutch underground during their search. The Ten Booms were imprisoned. Corrie and her sister Betsie spent 10 months in three different prisons, the last was the infamous Ravensbrück concentration camp near Berlin, Germany. Betsie died there, but Corrie was eventually freed.

Corrie received many tributes. She was knighted by the Queen of Holland. Her story became a bestselling book called *The Hiding Place*.

In the 1970s Corrie's book *The Hiding Place* became a bestseller and was even turned into a movie.

Corrie showing the entrance to the hiding place (left), and view from inside (right).

President Franklin Delano Roosevelt sent William Donovan on a secret mission. Officially, Donovan was a wealthy lawyer involved in politics. But he led a secret double life as a spy. In June 1940, he was asked to check the situation in Great Britain. Others had told the president that Britain could not repel an attack from Nazi Germany.

Major Donovan reported back that Britain could fight on, but needed American help. The U.S. had not yet joined the war directly. Donovan then went on secret missions to Italy to report on its dictator, Mussolini.

Soon the president trusted Major Donovan to form a special agency, the Office of Strategic Services (O.S.S.). Its people would work in secret abroad. Major Donovan built a team of 16,000 agents working behind enemy lines. He was known by reporters as "The Spymaster." His agents were responsible for espionage and for helping the resistance movements in occupied Europe.

Donovan during WWI.

Eileen Nearne
code name: Agent Rose

Eileen Nearne was an agent for England's Special Operations Executive. She parachuted into France, where her perfect French allowed her to hide her British identity. Her alias was Mademoiselle du Tort. She worked as a radio operator and helped coordinate resistance fighters and Allied spies against the Nazis.

Eventually she was captured and sent to prison, but she escaped along with two daring French women and made her way to American troops.

Nancy Wake
code name: The White Mouse

Nancy Wake was such a good British agent that the Nazis put her on their "Most Wanted" list. She planned and executed a raid on a Gestapo fort and an arms factory in France in 1944. She always eluded capture, and saved the lives of hundreds of resistance workers. She earned medals from the British, French, and American governments, and from Australia, where she grew up.

Australian spy Nancy Wake during the war (left) and in 2004.

Virginia Hall
code name: Marie of Lyon, or Artemis

Virginia Hall was an American who worked for Major Donovan's O.S.S. The Gestapo feared her as one of the most dangerous Allied spies. They called her "The Limping Lady" and thought she was an old Frenchwoman. Her disguise was perfect. She pretended to be old, just as years earlier she posed as a journalist. She coordinated the work of the French underground. She helped prisoners of war and downed Allied airmen to safety. She even led sabotage attacks on bridges and Nazi convoys. When the war ended, she spent the rest of her life working as a secret agent for the U.S.

Virginia Hall's many passports for her various secret identities.

Bletchley Park looked like a run-down English manor house from the outside. Inside, people worked night and day to break enemy codes.

Messenger Girl

When 14-year-old Mimi Gallilee was hired at the English estate called Bletchley Park, she didn't even know what the job would be. But the first thing she had to do was sign and swear an oath of secrecy. She wasn't allowed to tell anyone about Bletchley Park or what she did there.

Mimi's job turned out to be delivering mail and other messages to the people working in the buildings on the estate.

The top-secret work of Bletchley Park, as Mimi eventually discovered, was code-breaking. Thousands of people worked in the Bletchley huts in shifts, 24 hours a day. They cracked German codes, translated enemy messages, and sent the information to Allied commanders. The decoded messages were vital in defeating the enemy. American General (and later President) Dwight Eisenhower said that the code-breaking work at Bletchley Park shortened World War II by two years.

Allied spies used code scarfs to read coded messages.

29 USA

Allies decipher secret enemy codes, 1942

WHO'S GOOD AT CRACKING CODES?

Some of the Bletchley Park code-breakers and translators were mathematicians or language experts. But others were historians, expert chess players, and even crossword-puzzle whizzes.

Information about the code-breaking work at Bletchley Park was kept secret until the 1970s.

The Prof and the Enigma

Alan Turing worked at Bletchley Park, where he was known as "the Prof." He was a mathematical genius and the best cryptologist, or code-breaker, of World War II.

The Germans encoded their military messages with a machine called the Enigma. The Enigma code was fiercely difficult to crack. Not only did the code change with every letter in a message, but the Germans changed the settings on the machines every day. There were millions and millions of possible combinations.

The Bletchley code-breakers knew how the Enigma worked, but that wasn't any good unless they could figure out the settings for a particular day. Alan Turing designed a decoding machine called a "bombe" (named after an earlier Polish machine). The clicking, whirring bombe could figure out Enigma settings in a fraction of the time it would take a person to do it.

Alan Turing (above) and his decoding machine, the bombe.

THE LITTLE SHIPS OF DUNKIRK

Ken Horner was a 17-year-old sailor and fisherman. He worked aboard a small fleet of boats called bawleys. The 40-foot bawleys fished for little clams called cockles in the River Thames near London, England.

On May 30, 1940, the crews got a message that the British Royal Navy needed their bawleys for an important mission. They were to set sail that night for Dunkirk, France.

Ken Horner's crewmates told him he was too young for the dangerous trip. Ken didn't let that stop him. He ran home to get permission from his mother, then chased after the bawleys on his bicycle. He caught up with his fleet two miles away.

A London fireboat returning from the Dunkirk rescue (above). British troops waiting to be evacuated on the beaches at Dunkirk (left).

Ships reenacting Operation Dynamo in 2010.

Operation Dynamo

That night the six bawleys set sail in a convoy across the English Channel, under the command of a Navy lieutenant. They were part of Operation Dynamo, a rescue plan to save hundreds of thousands of soldiers who were surrounded by the German army. The British and French forces were cut off, and their only escape was across the Channel through Dunkirk.

The Navy needed every boat they could get. They put out a call for all merchant, fishing, and private boats. Most were taken over by Navy sailors, but some, like the six bawleys, brought their own crews.

The boats braved the Channel crossing, enduring air attacks by German dive bombers, and reached France. At Dunkirk, Ken Horner's bawley and hundreds of other little boats made trip after trip, ferrying soldiers from the teeming beaches to large ships offshore.

Over a week, the sailors and ships of Operation Dynamo evacuated more than 300,000 soldiers to England. This massive rescue could never have happened without the miracle of the little ships.

The evacuation was front-page news (above). The crew from a French ship sunk by a mine at Dunkirk had to be rescued by a British vessel (left).

HE SURVIVED!

Among the little ships was the *Sundowner*, a 58-foot yacht. Her captain was Charles Lightoller. Twenty-eight years before Operation Dynamo, Lightoller himself had survived a dramatic sea rescue. He was the second officer on the *Titanic*!

Lightoller managed to pack 130 soldiers and sailors into the *Sundowner*, which normally carried at most 21 people. One of the crew wondered if it was a good idea to be sailing with a man who went down with the *Titanic*. His friend answered, "No, he's the right fellow. He survived!"

Charles Dryden's Dream

Charles Dryden always wanted to fly. As a boy in New York City he spent hours building rubber-band-powered model airplanes out of balsa wood and tissue paper. In college, he signed up for pilot training and earned a pilot's license. At the age of 20, Charles Dryden could fly real planes!

Charles Dryden during his training as a fighter pilot.

Charles didn't just want to fly airplanes, he wanted to fly the fastest planes around: the fighters of the U.S. Army Air Corps. But there was a problem. Charles Dryden was a Jamaican American. When he went to the recruiting office to apply, the sergeant told him, "The United States Army isn't training any Colored pilots," and sent him away.

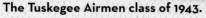
The Tuskegee Airmen class of 1943.

The Tuskegee Airmen

There had been African American aviators since the earliest days of flight, but the Army Air Corps never allowed them to become military pilots. It wasn't until 1940 that President Franklin Roosevelt ordered the Air Corps to form an all-African-American flying unit. The Army set up a flight training center in Tuskegee, Alabama. The pilots who trained there became known as the Tuskegee Airmen.

The Tuskegee program came just in time for Charles Dryden. A month after his first try, he went back to the recruiting office. This time the sergeant gave him an application. Charles was accepted for air training at the Tuskegee flying school, and in the spring of 1942, Second Lieutenant Charles Dryden earned his silver wings as a fighter pilot.

Lt. Dryden went to war with the first squadron of Tuskegee Airmen in 1943. They flew missions from North Africa across the Mediterranean Sea to battle the German *Luftwaffe* over Italy.

By the end of World War II, nearly a thousand Tuskegee Airmen had earned their wings. Four fighter squadrons flew missions over Europe, including 179 missions escorting bombers far into enemy territory. In all of their escort missions, the Tuskegee Airmen lost only seven bombers to enemy attack.

Keep us flying!

BUY WAR BONDS

Benjamin O. Davis in front of his plane (left). The Tuskegee Airmen Congressional Medal of Honor (above).

PEARL HARBOR

On December 7, 1941, the Japanese Imperial Navy attacked the U.S. naval base at Pearl Harbor, Hawaii. It was a sneak attack during which 353 Japanese planes killed 2,402 Americans. Japan was part of the Axis powers. Japanese forces believed that America would interfere with Japan's plan to take over territories in Southeast Asia. The Japanese attacked Pearl Harbor to prevent the U.S. Pacific fleet from getting involved.

A Date Which Will Live in Infamy

Up until this point, many felt the U.S. should stay out of the war. An attack on home turf changed people's minds. The next day, President Franklin D. Roosevelt declared war on Japan, and soon American troops were fighting in both the Pacific and Europe. President Roosevelt called December 7, 1941 "a date which will live in infamy."

...we here highly resolve that these dead shall not have died in vain...

REMEMBER DEC. 7th!

29 USA

Japanese bomb Pearl Harbor, December 7

The explosions in Pearl Harbor following the Japanese attack.

The U.S.S. *Arizona* Memorial

Over a thousand sailors and Marines lost their lives on the U.S.S. *Arizona* during the attack on Pearl Harbor. The sunken battleship was turned into a memorial to honor their sacrifice. The memorial was built over the sunken hull of the battleship and is accessible only by boat. Over a million people visit every year.

The U.S.S. *Arizona* rests just below the surface in Pearl Harbor.

The Japanese surrender on the deck of U.S.S. *Missouri* on September 2, 1945.

In 1999, the battleship U.S.S. *Missouri* was moved to Pearl Harbor to be docked next to the Arizona Memorial. On September 2, 1945, the Japanese surrendered to U.S. General Douglas MacArthur on the deck of the U.S.S. *Missouri* in Tokyo Bay. This surrender marked the end of World War II. The two ships thus represent the beginning and end of World War II for the United States.

PHILADELPHIA
DEC. 11 1941
P.A.

Cornelia Fort

Cornelia Fort was a 22-year-old flight teacher in Honolulu, Hawaii. Early one morning in December, she sat behind her student in the cockpit of a Piper Cub. The student pilot was taking the plane down for a landing. Suddenly, Cornelia saw a military airplane headed straight for their tiny Cub. She grabbed the controls and pulled the Cub into a climb. The other plane roared past below, missing them by a hair. On top of its wings, Cornelia saw the red sun emblem of Japan.

Cornelia looked over at nearby Pearl Harbor. Smoke billowed into the air. Shiny silver planes filled the sky overhead. She watched in horror as a bomb fell from the belly of one plane and exploded in the middle of the harbor. Cornelia quickly brought the Cub down to safety.

In the fall of 1942, Cornelia got a telegram inviting her to apply for the new Women's Auxiliary Ferrying Squadron, or WAFS. The squadron would fly military planes within the country, for example taking them from aircraft factories to air bases. Cornelia Fort jumped at the chance to serve her country. She joined the squad of 28 original WAFS, the first female pilots ever to fly for the U.S. military.

Cornelia Forts

Flight log book showing Cornelia Fort's December 7, 1941 flight.

The WASP uniform featured their mascot, Fifinella, on the lapel.

The WASPs

It took some convincing to get the military to accept women pilots. The woman who did the convincing was Jacqueline "Jackie" Cochran. When the military finally allowed women to fly, there were two groups: the WAFS and the Women's Flying Training Detachment, or WFTD. Eventually the two were combined into the Women's Airforce Service Pilots, or WASPs, under Jackie Cochran's command.

WASP pilots flew every kind of airplane the Army Air Forces used, from tiny trainers to fighter planes and giant bombers. Along with ferrying planes from place to place, they taught new pilots, tested planes, towed flying targets for gunnery practice (with live ammunition!), flew in practice dogfights, and even rode as backup pilots in some of the first radio-controlled drone aircraft.

ANNAPOLIS
OCT.
27
9:00 AM
1945
MD.

Jackie Cochran in the cockpit.

Don't miss your great opportunity..

THE NAVY NEEDS YOU IN THE WAVES

This is the team that's sweeping the seas

ENLIST IN THE WAVES TODAY

Share the Deeds of Victory

Join the WAVES

NAVY RECRUITING STATION OR OFFICE OF NAVAL OFFICER PROC

WESTERN UNION

U.S. NAVY

THAT WAS THE DAY I JOINED THE WAVES

INQUIRE AT ANY
Navy Recruiting Station or Office of Naval Officer Procurement

JOIN UP

Recruiting posters for WAVES, the female division of the U.S. Navy.

• ALLIED •

SUPERMARINE SPITFIRE

The Supermarine Spitfire was used by Britain's Royal Air Force, and by many other Allied countries. This single-engine fighter plane defended against enemy bombers, but also did reconnaissance missions.

• ALLIED •

P-51 MUSTANG

The P-51 Mustang is an American fighter plane. It was designed to be used on long-range missions. In World War II, the U.S. Air Force used P-51s as escort bombers in raids over Germany.

• ALLIED •

YAKOVLEV YAK-3

The Yak-3 is a Soviet fighter plane. It was small and light, and pilots loved it. It was used in dogfights—aerial combat—and for flying low over battlefields.

MESSERSCHMITT BF 109

This German fighter plane was used early in the war. It was the backbone of Germany's *Luftwaffe*, or Air Force. More BF 109s were produced than nearly any other aircraft in history. Nearly 34,000 planes were built between 1936 and 1941.

• AXIS •

MESSERSCHMITT ME 262

Also called the *Schwalbe* (German for "swallow"), the ME 262 was the world's first jet-powered fighter plane. Germany's *Luftwaffe* began using it in 1944. It was so much faster than Allied aircraft that Allied forces targeted it while it was on the ground or during takeoff and landing.

• AXIS •

MITSUBISHI A6M ZERO

Mitsubishi A6M Zeros were used by the Imperial Japanese Navy. This plane was designed as a carrier fighter—for taking off and landing on large warships. The Zero was meant for long-range flying and was used in dogfights. Later in the war it was used in kamikaze missions (suicide missions meant to destroy Allied warships).

On December 7, 1941, Yoshiko Uchida and her family heard an urgent voice break in to the radio program they were listening to. The announcer said Japan had attacked the American navy base in Pearl Harbor, Hawaii.

The same Sunday as the Japanese attack, American secret agents from the FBI took Yoshiko's father away for questioning. He and hundreds of other Japanese-American leaders were moved to a prisoner of war camp in Montana.

In the panic following Pearl Harbor, especially on the West Coast, some in the U.S. government became suspicious of all Japanese and Japanese Americans.

Yoshiko Uchida and her family at the Topaz internment camp in 1943.

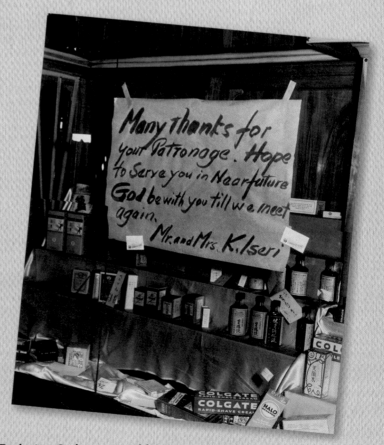

Exclusion Order 9066 told Japanese Americans to report for relocation. People had to close up their homes and businesses and leave their lives behind.

Interned

To their shame and horror, Yoshiko, her sister, and her mother were forced to leave their sunny home in Berkeley, California, and all their belongings, including their dog, Laddie. They stayed at first in the horse stalls at a racetrack. Then they were moved to an internment camp called Topaz in Utah.

Conditions were terrible. Life was so miserable, that the Japanese Americans felt like prisoners in a concentration camp—in the United States.

Yoshiko Uchida wrote several books about her experience. "Each time I find it hard to believe that this happened in the United States," she wrote. "I find it painful to continue remembering and writing about it. But I must."

Yoshiko hopes that if people are informed and careful, such a tragedy will never happen to a group of people again.

A little girl waiting for the bus to the internment camp.

FIRST, SECOND, THIRD

In Japanese culture, each generation has a name. These names are derived from the numbers "one, two, three" in the Japanese language—"ichi, ni, san."

- **Issei:** Born in Japan, the Issei are people who moved to the United States and became Japanese-American.
- **Nisei:** Born in the United States, the Nisei were the sons and daughters of Japanese immigrants, the Issei.
- **Sansei:** The Sansei are the grandchildren of Issei. Sansei are born in the United States just as their parents were, but their grandparents were born in Japan.

Scenes from life in the internment camps. People organized to grow their own food, start schools, and try to resume their lives despite their circumstances.

DANIEL INOUYE AND THE NISEI SOLDIERS

Daniel Inouye

Daniel Inouye (pronounced in-NO-ay) was a 17-year-old medical volunteer at Pearl Harbor when the Japanese planes attacked in December, 1941. Born in Hawaii, Daniel was a *nisei*, an American-born child whose parents were from Japan. After the attack he wanted to join the Army. But the Army banned Japanese Americans from serving, mistakenly believing they would all be loyal to the enemy.

Then finally the Army lifted the ban in 1943. They asked for volunteers for a new all-nisei unit, the 442nd Regimental Combat Team. They wanted 1,500 nisei soldiers from Hawaii. More than 10,000 volunteered. One of them was Daniel Inouye.

As he left Hawaii for Army training on the mainland, his father said to him, "America has been good to us. We owe a lot to this country, and if you must give your life, so be it. Whatever you do, do not dishonor your family or your nation."

A LIFE OF SERVICE

Daniel Inouye served his country for his entire life. After the war, he studied law and became a prosecutor. Soon he was elected to Hawaii's territorial legislature (Hawaii wasn't a state yet). Then, when Hawaii became a state in 1959, he was elected to be the state's first U.S. congressman. Daniel Inouye was elected to the U.S. Senate in 1962. He served there for almost 50 years, until his death in 2012.

The 442nd Regimental Combat Team was the most decorated military unit of its size in the history of the United States. But because of prejudice against Japanese Americans, none of the nisei soldiers received the country's highest military award, the Medal of Honor. In the year 2000, 22 of the unit's Distinguished Service Cross medals were upgraded to the Medal of Honor, including Daniel Inouye's.

Nisei soldiers on the Congressional Medal of Honor.

Troops in the 442nd standing at attention (above). Nisei soldier Harry Koba (right).

Go For Broke!

The 442nd Regimental Combat Team included nisei soldiers from Hawaii as well as from the mainland. The mainland nisei volunteered to serve their country, even though that same country had mistrusted them, taken them from their homes, and put them into internment camps. The regiment's motto was "Go for broke!" It means to risk everything for a big achievement. The nisei soldiers did just that as they fought to victory in Europe.

Iwo Jima is a small island, only a few miles across, about 750 miles south of Tokyo. There was a Japanese air base on the island. On February 19, 1945, the U.S. Marines invaded Iwo Jima.

The photo of the flag raising on Iwo Jima is one of the most famous images of World War II.

The Picture that Captured the Hope of a Nation

On the fourth day of the Battle of Iwo Jima, a platoon of marines carried a small flag to the top of Mt. Suribachi, a 556-foot volcano on the southern tip of the island. They used a long water pipe for a flagpole. Afterwards, they fought a small skirmish with two Japanese soldiers at the summit.

Later that day, the colonel in charge of the marines on the mountain sent a runner named Rene Gagnon to carry up a bigger flag. The colonel wanted every person on the island to be able to see it. Gagnon met four other marines on the way. Joined by a sixth man at the top, they worked together to raise the second flag on Mt. Suribachi.

War photographer Joe Rosenthal caught the scene on film. When the photo reached the United States, it became an instant symbol of America's hope and determination in the war.

The battle of Iwo Jima continued for more than three weeks after the flag went up. When the fighting was over, tens of thousands of Americans and Japanese had been killed or wounded, including three of the four men in the photo.

Iwo Jima Memorial honors the soldiers who lost their lives there.

The Men Who Raised the Flag

Sergeant Michael Strank

Mike Strank was born in Czechoslovakia. He came to the U.S. when his parents emigrated to Pennsylvania. He enlisted in the Marines in 1939, before the war started. He lost his life to a mortar shell six days after the photo was taken.

Private First Class Ira Hayes

Ira Hayes was a Native American of the Pima tribe from Arizona. Like Rene Gagnon, Ira Hayes didn't finish high school. Before enlisting in the Marines he was a carpenter.

Corporal Harlon Block

Harlon Block was from Texas. He was drafted into the Marines after high school. Harlon Block also died in the fighting six days after raising the flag.

Private First Class Franklin Sousley

Frank Sousley grew up in Kentucky and moved to Ohio after high school. He was drafted into the Marines in 1944. Sousley lost his life just a few days before the battle ended.

Private First Class Rene Gagnon

Rene Gagnon grew up in New Hampshire, where he worked in a textile factory after dropping out of high school. He signed up for the Marines in 1943 at the age of 18.

Pharmacist's Mate John Bradley

John Bradley was from Wisconsin. He was a Navy corpsman, one of the medics who treat wounded U.S. Marines in battle. Bradley was badly wounded eight days after the flag raising.

NAVAJO CODE TALKERS

A message for "Arizona" or "New Mexico" was the signal for a Navajo code talker to go to work.

"Message for Arizona"

Around noon on February 23, 1945, during the Battle of Iwo Jima, a voice came over the two-way radio: "Message for Arizona." Nineteen-year-old Private Sam Tso ran to relay the message. To most people the words that came next were a foreign language: "Dibeh shi-da dah-nas-tsah tkin shush wol-la-chee moasi lin yeh-hes." But to Sam they were his mother tongue, the language of the Diné (di-NEH), also known as the Navajo people.

Navajo code talkers in action in the South Pacific.

Code Talker

Samuel Tso was born in the Navajo Nation, near the Arizona–New Mexico border. He grew up speaking Navajo. For high school, Sam was sent to a U.S. government boarding school. The students there had to speak, read, and write only in English. They were punished for using their own language!

After high school, Sam lied about his age so he could get a job with the railroad. But this lie made him old enough to be drafted into the Marines. In the military, all of a sudden they *wanted* him to speak Navajo. He joined the group of Diné marines called code talkers. They used a code based on Navajo to send secret messages that the enemy couldn't decipher. Even their fellow marines couldn't understand the language. They often mistook Navajo radio transmissions for Japanese.

There were more than 400 Navajo code talkers in the U.S. Marine Corps. They took part in every battle in the Pacific war, including Iwo Jima. Marine Major Howard Connor said later, "Were it not for the Navajos, the Marines would never have taken Iwo Jima!"

Samuel Tso

THE NAVAJO CODE

The Diné code talkers didn't just send messages in Navajo. They used a special code based on that language. The first code talkers came up with a list of Navajo words to use for more than 200 military words in English. Later, another 200 words were added to the list. The code talkers had to memorize them all.

A code talker using a radio transmitter.

THE ANGELS OF BATAAN AND CORREGIDOR

A propaganda poster featuring a soldier from Bataan.

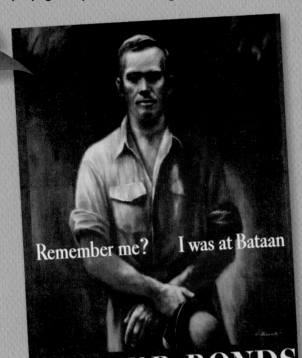

A propaganda poster featuring a soldier from Bataan.

Remember me?   I was at Bataan

BUY WAR BONDS

Deep in the jungle, thousands of hospital beds filled with wounded soldiers were spread out in all directions on the rainforest floor. Branches and vines formed the only roof. These were the open-air wards of Army Hospital No. 2 on the Bataan Peninsula, on the main island of Luzon in the Philippines. Close by, a battle raged as the Americans made a last stand against the Japanese.

First Lieutenant Josie Nesbit was the head nurse at Hospital No. 2. Most of the 72 nurses in her charge were in the Army. Some were Filipinas and other civilians. The soldiers called them the Angels of Bataan.

The battle went on for weeks. The American forces were trapped in Bataan and on a small nearby island called Corregidor. As Josie and the other nurses worked in surgery or cared for wounded patients in the wards, enemy planes roared right over the hospital.

NURSES QUARTERS
PLEASE RING
BEFORE ENTERING

Lt. Josie Nesbit and other Army nurses in Bataan (above). The jungle of Bataan (left).

Surrender

On April 8, 1942, the colonel in charge of the hospital told Josie to get all the American nurses together. They would be taken to safety on Corregidor. Josie refused to go unless she could take the Filipina nurses too. All 72 nurses went to Corregidor. The Americans surrendered Bataan the next day.

On Corregidor, the Angels worked in a hospital in a tunnel deep underground. Japanese bombs and cannons pounded the island. The Army held out on the island for another month, but help still didn't arrive. On May 6, 1942, the United States surrendered Corregidor and all of the Philippines to Japan.

Thousands of prisoners taken in Bataan were marched 80 miles to a prison camp. They were beaten and starved. It was one of the darkest moments of the war.

Finally Rescued!

Josie Nesbit and the other nurses spent the next three years in a civilian prison camp in Manila. As the Japanese began to lose the war, the food ran out. People starved. The nurses got very sick, and some nearly died. Finally, on February 3, 1945, an American tank came crashing through the prison gates. The Angels of Bataan and Corregidor were free.

American Army nurses after being rescued.

Susan Therp watched with pride as the champagne bottle smashed on the prow of the towering ship. The steel hull, as long as five football fields, slid slowly out of the dry dock and into the water. The *Sea Cardinal* was afloat, and Susan was one of the workers who built her.

Susan was 14 years old when the Japanese attacked Pearl Harbor. Her older brother left home to join the Navy. Later her father did, too. One day, when she was almost 17, Susan and a friend went to apply for jobs at the shipyard in South San Francisco. The Navy needed thousands of ships, and factories all over the country were hiring workers to build them. She was too young to work at the shipyard, but Susan told them she was 18. She got a job right away.

Susan became a welder. Before the war, it was a job done only by men. The work was challenging, and she liked it a lot. She was excited to do her part to help end the war and bring the soldiers and sailors home.

Susie Therp (top). A welder's certification card like Susie would have carried (above).

A machinists' union booklet and shipbuilding worker's badge.

"Soldiers without guns"

When the United States entered the war, the country started a huge effort to make planes, ships, tanks, trucks, weapons, and other equipment for the military. Millions of workers were needed. Before the war (and unlike today), only men did many of the jobs, in factories and other places. But with so many working-age men off fighting, there weren't enough of them to fill the jobs. Women stepped in to do the work. Newspaper and magazine articles of the time pointed out that the women were just as good at their jobs as men.

29 USA

Millions of women join war effort, 1942

Women did everything from build airplanes to make weapons.

The more WOMEN at work the sooner we WIN!

WOMEN ARE NEEDED ALSO AS:

FARM WORKERS	WAITRESSES	TIMEKEEPERS	LAUNDRESSES
TYPISTS	BUS DRIVERS	ELEVATOR OPERATORS	TEACHERS
SALESPEOPLE	TAXI DRIVERS	MESSENGERS	CONDUCTORS

—and in hundreds of other war jobs!

SEE YOUR LOCAL U.S. EMPLOYMENT SERVICE

A teen boy at work in an aircraft factory.

It wasn't just women who went to work when the men were called up to fight. Teenagers also did factory work, along with other jobs. By the spring of 1944, there were more than 3 million workers between the ages of 14 and 18 in the United States. Many of them had dropped out of high school to get jobs. The U.S. started a back-to-school drive in 1944 to get the teens to go back and finish school.

ROSIE THE RIVETER

In 1943 a popular vocal group called the Four Vagabonds recorded a song about a young woman working in an airplane factory. Her name was Rosie the Riveter.

Soon after, the artist Norman Rockwell painted a cover for the *Saturday Evening Post*. It showed a factory worker on her lunch break with her rivet gun resting across her lap. Her name was written on her lunch box: "Rosie."

The original Rosie the Riveter.

Women factory workers in action.

ROHR FORM NO. 40A

ROHR AIRCRAFT CORPORATION
CHULA VISTA, CALIFORNIA

PASS   Sex. Female

Name. Lillian Haws

Height. 5-2   Weight. 111

Hair. Brown   Eyes. Blue

EMPLOYEE'S SIGNATURE

Issued. 7-24-44

COMPANY OFFICIAL SIGNATURE

Many women felt proud to serve their country and tackle tough jobs once thought to only be for men.

We Can Do It!

The image everyone now knows as Rosie the Riveter appeared in a poster by J. Howard Miller. It shows Rosie in her factory coveralls, her hair tied up in a scarf to keep it from getting caught in the machinery. She's rolled up her sleeve to show her muscles, saying, "We can do it!"

Rosie the Riveter became a symbol of American women at work, doing their part to get the job done and help win the war.

The "We Can Do It!" poster was made for the Westinghouse company before the Four Vagabonds' song ever came out. It was only later that Rosie's name got attached to the woman in the poster.

At the end of the war, most women were expected to leave their wartime jobs so the returning men could have them back. It was more than a quarter century before women started working in many traditional "men's" jobs again.

LIFE AT HOME

Even though the fighting was far away, life for people at home changed when the country went to war. The military needed huge amounts of equipment and supplies. Factories needed raw materials to make the equipment. Soldiers, sailors, and pilots needed food and clothes. The people at home made do with less so the people fighting overseas could have what they needed.

Saving and Salvaging

People didn't say, "Reduce, reuse, recycle," in the 1940s, but the idea was the same. Drivers formed carpools and driving clubs to save fuel. Families crushed their empty tin cans and turned them in for recycling. Children collected scrap metal and rubber for the war effort. People even donated old cooking fat. The fat contained glycerin, which was used for making explosives.

SAVE SCRAP FOR VICTORY!
Save **METALS**
Save **PAPER**
Save **RUBBER**
Save **RAGS**

Kids delivering scrap rubber, paper, and metal to civilian defense headquarters.

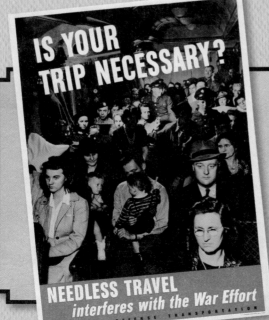

IS YOUR TRIP NECESSARY?

NEEDLESS TRAVEL interferes with the War Effort

OFFICE OF DEFENSE TRANSPORTATION

SLOW DOWN FOR VICTORY

The "victory speed" on all roads in the country was 35 miles per hour. The slower speed saved gas, but the biggest reason to slow down was to save rubber tires. Most rubber comes from Asia, and the war with Japan had cut off America's rubber supply. (The rubber shortage also meant doing without balloons at birthday parties!)

A Fair Share at a Fair Price

With so many supplies and raw materials needed for the military, many foods and other resources became scarce at home. The country started *rationing*, or limiting the amount of some things that each person could buy. The government also set a "ceiling price," or the highest price that sellers were allowed to charge. Rationing gave everyone a fair share of the scarce items. The ceiling price made sure that everyone had a chance to buy them, not just the people with the most money.

The government issued ration books for everyone, both adults and children. The books contained stamps that the buyer had to give along with money to pay for rationed items. Rationed goods included meat, dairy products, canned fruits and vegetables, sugar, coffee, shoes, tires, gasoline, and more.

Children shopping with their ration cards in hand (right). A ration card booklet (below).

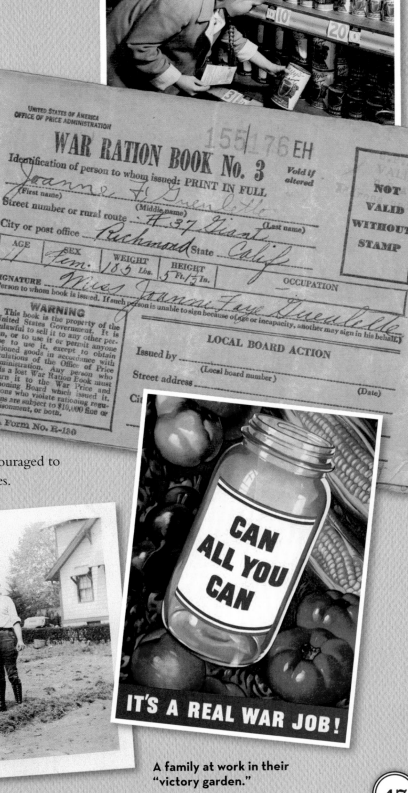

Victory Gardens

Everyone with even a tiny amount of space was encouraged to plant a "victory garden" to grow their own vegetables.

A family at work in their "victory garden."

CAN ALL YOU CAN

IT'S A REAL WAR JOB!

Rationing and shortages even affected the style of wartime clothes. Wool, nylon, rubber, leather, and other materials were needed for the military.

In 1942 the U.S. War Production Board put out a set of rules called Limitation Order L–85. The regulations gave clothing makers rules about the styles they could use. Baggy sleeves, wool linings, wide belts, and heavy cloth were all banned. Features that used extra layers of wool were also out, such as patch pockets, folded cuffs, and aprons.

Since the silk used to make stockings was rationed, women drew fake stocking seams on their legs.

The War Production Board even had rules for swimsuits. Swimwear makers were told to use 10% less cloth in their women's suits, so some of them took it out of the middle. The two-piece suit was born!

The first two-piece bathing suits were created to save fabric for the war effort.

Suit Yourself

The men's "Victory Suit" was designed to save wool and other materials for the war effort. Men's suits before the war often came with a vest and two pairs of pants. The Victory Suit got rid of the vest and did without the extra pants. To save more material, suit makers shortened the jackets, narrowed the pants, and did away with pocket flaps, pleats, cuffs, and sleeve buttons. Instead of pure wool, the cloth was a blend of wool and synthetic yarn.

In the U.S. there were rules about how clothes could be made, but only shoes and other leather items were rationed. Things were different in Britain, where all clothing was rationed.

Men's and women's suit styles changed due to the garment restrictions brought on by the war.

Make It Do

To save material for the war effort, many people learned to make do with what they had instead of buying new things. A book titled *Make and Mend for Victory* gave tips on saving and reusing clothes. There were chapters about mending, altering, and making new clothes out of pieces of old ones. Because the men who were away at war wouldn't be needing their civilian clothes, there were instructions for making children's clothes out of men's shirts and jackets, and for converting a man's suit to a woman's.

People were encouraged to fix and reuse old clothes to save new fabric for the military.

Make and Mend

CONSUMER'S VICTORY PLEDGE

"As a consumer, in the total defense of democracy, my part to make my home, my community, ready, efficient, strong.

I will buy carefully — and I will not buy any the ceiling price, no matter how much I ma

I will take good care of the things I have — buy anything made from vital war materia get along without.

I will waste nothing — and I will take everything needed to win the war."

CONSUMER Office of I

It's up to you to keep the home fires burning, to see that you and your family stay easy-on-the-eyes. Fortunately, you can be patriotic and pretty both. It's easy to teach an old wardrobe new tricks, to resurrect the skele-

tons in y date. Cor and turn glint in stint to

TABLE OF CONT

Copyright 1942, The Spool Cotton Company

MAKE and **MEND**
FOR VICTORY ★ BOOK NO. S-10 ★ PRICE 10 CENTS

ALTERATIONS

MAKE OVER

ACCESSORIES

MENDING AND DARNING

During World War II all kinds of posters were used to remind people that everyone had a part in the war effort. There were posters for everything from keeping quiet—you never know who could be listening—to what to do in an air raid. "Propaganda" means the spreading of ideas.

Loose Lips!

Many posters reminded citizens not to talk about troops' comings or goings.

Uncle Sam Wants You

Posters called for men and women to enlist in the armed forces and do their part.

Jobs at Home

The war meant many people were needed to work in factories building weapons, aircraft, and other supplies used by the military.

Air Raid!

People practiced what do in an enemy attack. Air raid posters reminded people not to scream and to obey instructions.

In the spring of 1942, the Army began training animals for its war dog program, otherwise known as the K-9 Corps. Dogs in the K-9 Corps went through two or three months of training to become guards, scouts, messengers, or to sniff out land mines.

Dogs in the K-9 Corps served in many different units.

Chips, the War Dog

The most famous dog in the K-9 Corps was Chips, a German shepherd mix from Pleasantville, New York. Chips served as an Army sentry dog in North Africa and Europe. He once saved a group of soldiers by warning them of an ambush. Then he ran back through whizzing bullets with a phone cable attached to his collar, so the soldiers could contact their base for help.

On a beach in Sicily, Chips charged into a guard-post full of Italian soldiers who were shooting at the Americans. His attack forced all of the soldiers inside to surrender. Chips was wounded in the fight, but later that night he helped to capture another group of Italians. He was discharged from Army duty in 1945 and returned to his family in Pleasantville.

Chips, the war hero.

G.I. Joe

There is an official commendation for animal heroes, called the Dickin Medal. The medal is British, but it was awarded to one American animal hero: a carrier pigeon named G.I. Joe.

In 1943, British soldiers were on their way to attack an Italian village occupied by the Germans. American planes had orders to help by bombing the village beforehand. But the British soldiers got into the village ahead of schedule. Now they needed to send an urgent message to the Americans: Don't attack! But the message didn't get through.

In a last-ditch try, the British soldiers sent G.I. Joe off into the air with a message for the Americans. The pigeon flew nearly 20 miles in 20 minutes. He arrived at the American air base just as the bombers were about to take off! He saved the lives of more than 100 British soldiers.

Wojtek, the bear, was adopted by the Polish 22nd Transport Artillery Company (left). A kitten found on the battlefield at Iwo Jima (right).

A Beach Called Omaha

Jerry Markham stood in the flat-bottomed landing craft, crowded together with other men and equipment. Jerry belonged to a nine-man Naval Combat Demolition Unit, whose members were known as frogmen. The boxlike boat pushed through the waves toward a wide, flat beach with tall cliffs behind. The beach was code-named "Omaha." It was the morning of June 6, 1944: D-Day.

The landing craft grounded on sand at the low tide mark. Jerry was scared, but he knew thousands of others were depending on him.

The beach and water were lined with rows of deadly obstacles. There were sunken posts with mines at the tips, spiky steel "hedgehogs" that could rip the bottoms out of boats, 10-foot concrete pyramids, steel barricades, and log ramps lined with explosives. The frogmen's job was to blow them up, and clear safe paths to the beach for the thousands of boats that followed behind.

Jerry and the other frogmen cleared five main channels and parts of three others before the rising tide forced them to stop. More than half of the 190 frogmen at Omaha Beach were wounded or killed. Their sacrifice opened the way for the gigantic Allied invasion that drove Hitler's armies out of northwest France.

Mines and obstacles on the beaches of Normandy.

29 USA

Allies in Normandy, D-Day, June 6, 1944

Soldiers landing on the beaches on D-Day.

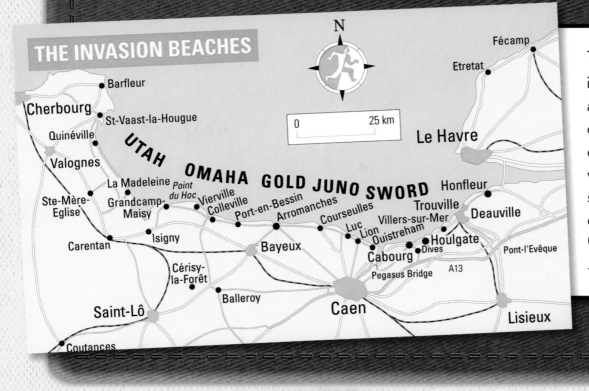

THE INVASION BEACHES

N

0   25 km

Fécamp
Etretat
Le Havre
Barfleur
Cherbourg
St-Vaast-la-Hougue
Quinéville
UTAH OMAHA GOLD JUNO SWORD
Valognes
La Madeleine Point du Hoc
Ste-Mère-Eglise Grandcamp-Maisy Vierville Colleville Port-en-Bessin Arromanches Courseulles Luc Villers-sur-Mer Honfleur Trouville Deauville
Carentan Isigny Bayeux Lion Ouistreham Houlgate Pont-l'Evêque
Cérisy-la-Forêt Cabourg Dives
Balleroy Pegasus Bridge A13
Saint-Lô Caen Lisieux
Coutances

The D-Day invasion took place across 18 miles of the Normandy coast. The beaches were divided into sections with code names Utah, Omaha, Gold, Juno, and Sword.

Operation Overlord

D-Day was the beginning of Operation Overlord, the Allied invasion of German–occupied France. More than 156,000 soldiers, airmen, and sailors fought for the beaches that day. More than 10,000 of them were wounded, killed, or captured.

With the beaches secure, nearly a third of a million Allied troops poured into Normandy. Over the next two months they drove the Germans back across the River Seine and freed Paris from enemy occupation. It was the first big strike in the fight that ended in German surrender 11 months later.

D-DAY
25p COMMANDOS LANDING ON GOLD BEACH 6 JUNE 1944

The Normandy Beach invasion was a turning point in the war.

LIBERATION

NAZIS SURRENDER HOLLAND, DENMARK AND NORTH REICH

When Staff Sergeant Al Kosiek led his platoon of 23 soldiers to the gates of the Mauthausen concentration camp in Austria, he could hardly believe his eyes. Behind an electric fence were hundreds of people who looked like living skeletons. But the starving prisoners cheered wildly when they saw the American soldiers.

The camp's guards led Sgt. Kosiek through the main gates. Inside were hundreds more cheering people. There were even three captured Americans, including a Navy captain! A band of prisoners played *The Star Spangled Banner*. The Navy captain had taught it to them the night before. Many of the now-free prisoners cried when they saw the soldiers standing at attention and saluting.

The next day, May 6, 1945, Colonel Richard Seibel rode into Mauthausen concentration camp at the head of the liberation force. A group of refugees came up and gave him an American flag. The prisoners had made it in secret out of old coats and sheets. The flag had 13 stripes, but there were 56 stars! The makers couldn't remember the right number of stars, and they had added an extra row. (There were 48 states at the time.) The Americans ran the 56-star flag up the flagpole, where it flew over the newly free camp.

Allies liberate Holocaust survivors, early 1945

A reproduction of the American flag sewn by prisoners (above). Newly liberated prisoners at Mauthausen (left).

Befinde mich ab *17 Sept* im Konzentrationslager Mauthausen (Oberdonau).

Meine Adresse: **Nur „Deutsch" schreiben**

Izaar Cohen No 5182

Geb 12 Maart 1908

1x im Monat Postempfang K.-L. Mauthausen (Oberdonau)

Block: *15* Stube: *a/*

Q 0176 4542 40

LeRoy "Pete" Petersohn was a 22-year-old Army medic in 1945. In the women's barracks at Mauthausen he found a mother with a three-week-old baby girl named Hana. The baby had infected sores and blisters all over her skin. If she didn't get medical help, she would die. LeRoy and his officer, a doctor, took the baby in a Jeep to the Army field hospital. The doctor treated Hana's sores while LeRoy cleaned them and put penicillin on them. For many years after the war he didn't know whether the baby had lived or died.

In 2005 LeRoy Petersohn returned to Austria for a celebration of the 60th anniversary of the liberation of Mauthausen. There, more than half a century after he had last seen her in person, LeRoy met Dr. Hana Berger Moran, the baby whose life he had helped to save.

LeRoy Petersohn and Hana reunited after 60 years.

Private Harry Ettlinger was just 18 years old when he stepped through the gates of Neuschwanstein (noy-SHVAN-shtine) Castle in the German Alps. It was May 1945, just weeks after the German surrender and the end of the war in Europe. There was treasure in the castle, room after room of it: gold, silver, jewels, furniture, and thousands of priceless paintings. And all of it had been stolen.

Harry Ettlinger was Jewish. He was born in Germany but escaped to the United States with his family before the war broke out. He was drafted into the Army after high school and sent back to the country of his birth. He had come to Neuschwanstein Castle with the U.S. Army's Monuments, Fine Arts, and Archives section (MFAA), also known as the Monuments Men.

Ettlinger (right) and another soldier inspect priceless pieces of art recovered after the war.

The job of the MFAA was to save as much of the cultural treasure of Europe as possible. That wasn't easy. The Allied forces had to bomb, shell, and shoot their way through towns and cities that were home to Europe's greatest buildings, monuments, and art. The Monuments Men followed the Army into battle. They checked important buildings and monuments for damage and arranged for repairs. They also made sure that the soldiers and inhabitants left the monuments alone afterward.

When the Germans surrendered, the Monuments men had another job: returning stolen art. The Nazis had looted art treasures from museums and the homes and galleries of Jewish collectors. They stored it for safekeeping in places like Neuschwanstein Castle and deep in underground mines.

Luckily, the Germans kept detailed records of their art thefts. Harry Ettlinger and the other Monuments men went to work, checking records, collecting art, and returning it to where it belonged.

The Germans hid art in many places, including the Altaussee salt mines (top). Sculptures being returned to the Louvre, after the war (right).

ART EVACUATION

As war loomed, Europe's great museums protected their collections from the bombs they knew were coming. At the Louvre in Paris, sculptures and paintings were crated up and sent away to the countryside in the south of France. The Mona Lisa, probably the most famous painting in the world, rode by itself in an ambulance with the windows sealed up to keep the proper humidity. The painting was safe, but the museum curator who rode with it fainted on the way.

The Mona Lisa was removed from the Louvre before the *blitzkrieg*.

John Lebda

Early on the morning of June 6, 1994, John Lebda stood on the deck of a ship off the coast of Normandy, France. It was the second time he had been there. The first time had been very different. Then, he had been crammed in a tossing, rolling landing craft full of vehicles and seasick soldiers on their way to the deadly sands of Omaha Beach.

John had returned to Europe along with tens of thousands of other veterans. They were there for the 50th anniversary of the D-Day invasion. He was aboard the U.S.S *George Washington* for a ceremony at sunrise that morning. President Bill Clinton placed a wreath in the water to honor those who had been lost at sea on D-Day. He thanked the veterans for changing the course of history at Normandy. Standing at attention in his old Army uniform, John saluted the president and shook his hand.

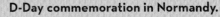

D-Day commemoration in Normandy.

Later he visited the cemetery overlooking Omaha Beach. Tears blurred his eyes as he walked among the graves of the soldiers who died on the beach that day, half a century before. Many of the stone crosses marked the resting places of his friends.

The next day John climbed up to the ruined German gun emplacements on the bluff behind the beach. At the top of the bluff was a monument to his division, the 1st Infantry, known as the Big Red One.

A monument for the 1st infantry at Omaha Beach (above), and a marker for a fallen soldier who died during the invasion (left).

JUMPING GRANDPAS

Some of the veterans at the D-Day anniversary arrived the way they had 50 years earlier, by parachute. More than a thousand paratroopers re-enacted the original D-Day drop. Thirty-eight of them were American veterans of the World War II, and 16 had jumped at the Normandy invasion. The oldest was 83-year-old Rene Dussaq. The French called them the *papys sauteurs*, or "jumping grandpas."

Paratroopers on D-Day.

TIMELINE OF WORLD WAR II

Oskar Schindler opens his factory in Krakow, Poland.

Germany invades Czechoslovakia in March.

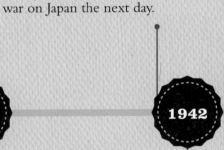

In September, Germany invades Poland.

Major William Donovan forms the Office of Strategic Services (O.S.S.).

On December 7, the Japanese bomb the naval base at Pearl Harbor, Hawaii. The United States declares war on Japan the next day.

1939　　**1940**　　**1941**　　**1942**

Hortense Clews joins the Belgian resistance.

1933: Adolf Hitler comes into power and forms the Nazi Party in Germany.

Germany wages *blitzkrieg* on Northern Europe. Denmark, the Netherlands, Belgium, Norway, and France all surrender in a matter of months.

On May 27-June 4, Operation Dynamo occurs. Ships evacuate over 300,000 soldiers from Dunkirk, France.

Charles Dryden begins his training as a Tuskegee airman.

On September 3, Britain, France, New Zealand, and Australia declare war on Germany.

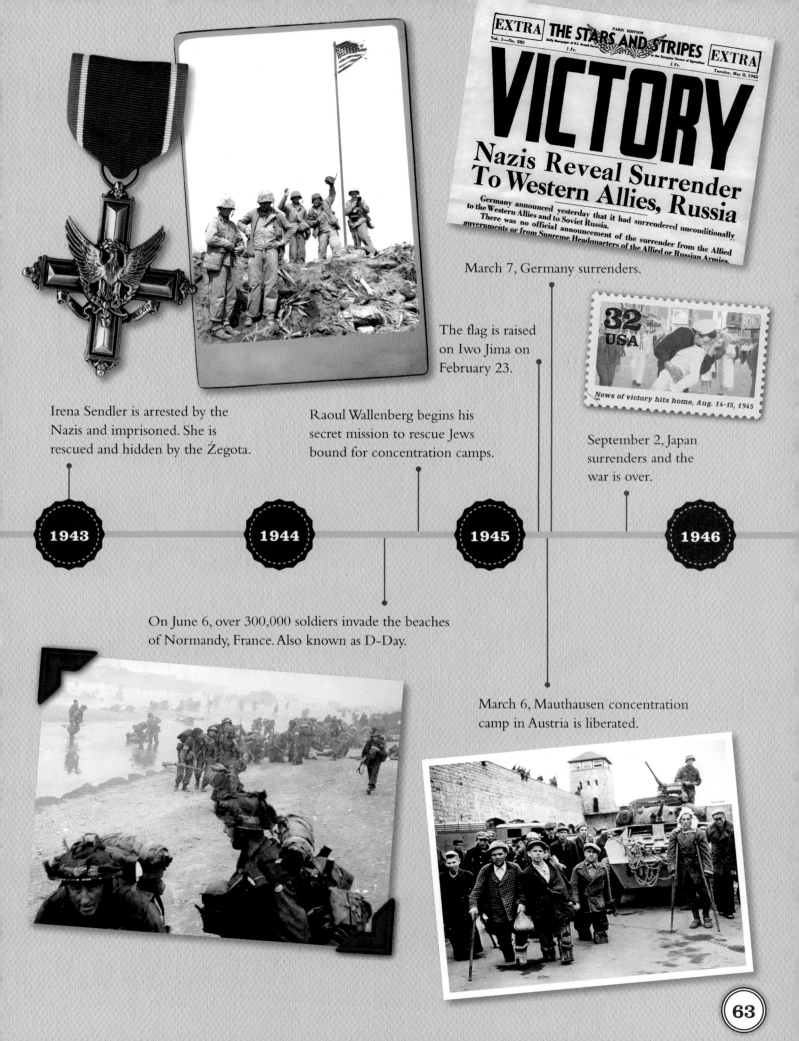

EXTRA THE STARS AND STRIPES **EXTRA**
PARIS EDITION
Vol. 1—No. 285
Daily Newspaper of U.S. Armed Forces
1 Fr.
in the European Theater of Operations
1 Fr.
Tuesday, May 8, 1945

VICTORY

Nazis Reveal Surrender To Western Allies, Russia

Germany announced yesterday that it had surrendered unconditionally, to the Western Allies and to Soviet Russia.
There was no official announcement of the surrender from the Allied governments or from Supreme Headquarters of the Allied or Russian Armies.

March 7, Germany surrenders.

The flag is raised on Iwo Jima on February 23.

32 USA

News of victory hits home, Aug. 14–15, 1945

September 2, Japan surrenders and the war is over.

Irena Sendler is arrested by the Nazis and imprisoned. She is rescued and hidden by the Żegota.

Raoul Wallenberg begins his secret mission to rescue Jews bound for concentration camps.

1943　　**1944**　　**1945**　　**1946**

On June 6, over 300,000 soldiers invade the beaches of Normandy, France. Also known as D-Day.

March 6, Mauthausen concentration camp in Austria is liberated.

AFTER THE WAR

Germany surrendered to the Allies in Europe on May 7, 1945. Nearly four months later, on the other side of the world, Japan surrendered on September 2. Finally the war was over. Thousands of heroes began returning home.

Some went back to "ordinary" lives. Resistance worker Hortense Clews lived quietly with her husband and children in England. Code Talker Samuel Tso became a teacher.

Others continued in lives of service after the war. Pilot Charles Dryden stayed in the Air Force, serving in Korea and reaching the rank of colonel. Daniel Inouye became one of the longest-serving members of the United States Senate.

Still others, like Raoul Wallenberg and Cornelia Fort, never returned. They gave their lives to end the war.

These heroes and many, many others truly saved the world from evil. Thanks to them, there has never been another world war.

The world celebrated the end of the war.

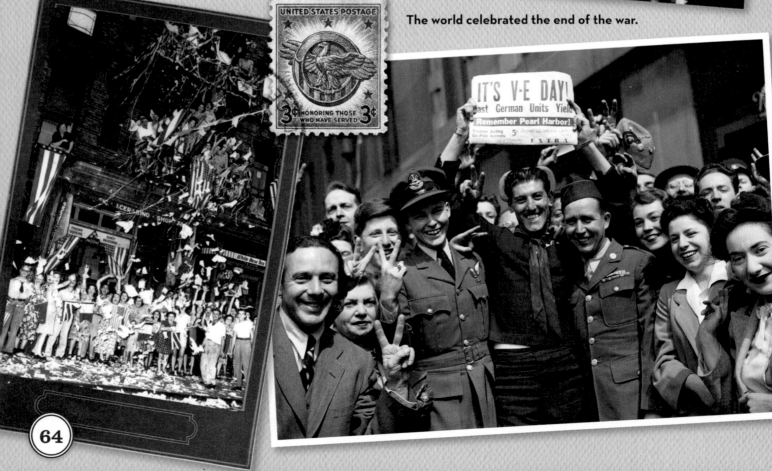